managing for
the first time

CHERRY MILL

Cherry Mill is European human resources manager for SGI – Silicon
Graphics and has 12 years' experience of human resources and management
in international commercial and not-for-profit organisations in many
countries. Cherry has a degree in modern languages from the University of
Oxford, a diploma in personnel management from the University of
Westminster and is a Member of the Chartered Institute of Personnel and
Development.

Management Shapers is a comprehensive series covering all the crucial management skill areas. Each book includes the key issues, helpful starting points and practical advice in a concise and lively style. Together, they form an accessible library reflecting current best practice – ideal for study or quick reference.

The Chartered Institute of Personnel and Development is the leading publisher of books and reports for personnel and training professionals, students, and all those concerned with the effective management and development of people at work. For full details of all our titles, please contact the Publishing Department:

tel. 020-8263 3387
fax 020-8263 3850
e-mail publish@cipd.co.uk

The catalogue of all CIPD titles can be viewed on the CIPD website:
www.cipd.co.uk/publications

managing for
the first time

CHERRY MILL

Chartered Institute of Personnel and Development

First published in 2000
Reprinted 2000

Design by Curve
Typesetting by Paperweight
Printed in Great Britain by
The Guernsey Press, Channel Islands

British Library Cataloguing in Publication Data
A catalogue record for this book is available from the
British Library

ISBN
0-85292-858-0

Chartered Institute of Personnel and Development, CIPD House,
Camp Road, London SW19 4UX
Tel.: 020 8971 9000   Fax: 020 8263 3333
E-mail: cipd@cipd.co.uk   Website: www.cipd.co.uk
Incorporated by Royal Charter. Registered charity no. 1079797

contents

Other titles in the series:

introduction

Common dilemmas for first-time managers

'How do I make a good first impression as a manager?'

'How do I manage someone who is a friend?'

'How do I manage someone who is older than I am?'

'How do I go from being one of us to one of them?'

'How do I develop the right leadership style?'

'How do I motivate people?'

'How do I start...?'

You've just got a new job as a manager. How do you feel? Elated, excited, energised, full of plans and ideas? But maybe with just a touch of panic? How are you going to handle it all?

Managing the transition to becoming a manager

Most people become a manager because they are good at what they do – but being a manager is a completely different job. Your success depends not just on how well you do your own job, but on how well you get things done through other people – because you can't do it all yourself, however many hours you work.

So you need to start developing a different set of skills, many of which will be completely new to you, and learn how to lead and manage others to help you achieve your goals.

How this book will help

This book will get you off to a great start, and help you manage your transition into the new role. It tells you how to:

● manage your crucial first 100 days

■ manage some of the typical challenges you will come across

▲ keep yourself motivated

● plan your development as a manager.

You can use it as a planning guide, as a checklist, or just to dip into for advice.

Although it's aimed at people managing for the first time, it also provides a good framework to use whenever you begin a new job as a manager and have to take on a new team or get off to an impressive start.

The principles apply whether you are supervising just one person or have a whole group to manage – it's all about how you deal with the individuals for whom you are responsible.

Because so much of your success as a manager depends on how effectively you lead your people, the book focuses on the people management challenges of becoming a new manager, rather than on the business or financial management aspects. There are plenty of other books on the market that look at those areas.

Learning from experience

A notable feature of the book is the feedback from over 30 managers about their experiences of managing for the first time. It draws on their challenges, their excitements, their successes and their failures – and brings together real practical advice on how to get off to a good start. You will see their contributions set as quotations in italics throughout the book, and I should like to acknowledge and thank them for their advice and insights.

The contributors are listed below. They come from seven countries – the UK, USA, France, Germany, Italy, Spain, and The Netherlands – and from a range of industries including IT, retail, fashion, film, publishing, energy, consultancy, law, tax, manufacturing, teaching, the health service – and management headhunting!

I am particularly grateful to colleagues from my own company SGI – Silicon Graphics, who made a huge contribution. Other organisations include Aspect Communications UK Ltd, Camenos, Consiel, the Council of Europe, DCS Group plc, Dorset Local Education Authority, EMC Computers,

F.S. Cargo Division Italy, Fulcrum Productions Ltd, House of Fraser, Institute of Directors, the CIPD, Novell Inc, Pixar Animation Studios, PricewaterhouseCoopers, the Tavistock and Portman NHS Trust, The Design Net, Third Age Media, TiVo, West Dorset Food and Land Trust and West Herts Community Health Trust.

The contributors are: Alethea Snelling, Andrew Cracknell, Andrew Spybey, Andrew Nind, Ann Pennell, Anne Cordwent, Christina Hughes, Colin Wilson, Dolores Rios, Drew Banks, Ed Martin, Elizabeth Monaghan, Giorgio Righetti, Heidi Pohl, Jackie Ellis, Joanne de Nobriga, John Henderson, Jonathan Rudge, Karrin Nicol, Katy Dearnley, Marinus ter Laak, Mark Rieland, Michelle Ney, Neil Crawford, Nick Foster, Richard Payne, Roger Cooper, Sarah Stenton, Simonetta Sorio, Stuart Lanyon, Tim Crabtree, Tim Robinson, Tracey Gardiner.

becoming a manager   1

What do managers do?

There are many books about managing people, but no universal overall definition of what being a people manager means – so here is a personal view of 10 activities that most managers do:

- *planning* how work gets done – what needs doing, which people are needed to do it, how to structure the team and divide up the tasks

- *recruiting* people with the right skills, knowledge, personality and potential to do the work now and in the future

- *training* and coaching people to do a good job, reach their goals and develop their abilities

- *developing* efficient working methods

- *agreeing* team plans and objectives, and individual plans and objectives, so that everyone knows what they are doing and why, and how it fits into the overall organisation

- *managing* the performance of each individual – setting quality standards, coaching, giving feedback, managing problems, doing performance reviews

■ *communicating* information to the team and communicating the team's work and ideas to the outside

▲ *ensuring* that people are paid fairly and competitively for their contribution, and that their efforts and achievements are recognised

● *managing* the team budget

● *managing change.*

All this is tactical – the day-to-day operational tasks that make up a large part of the responsibilities of a manager.

Then there is the more strategic aspect of being a manager, which is about having the ability to motivate people and inspire them to work towards the organisation's goals. This is leadership. All managers should be leaders, but not all leaders are managers.

If you are new to managing people, you will probably start by focusing on the operational challenges. The main part of the book (Chapter 2) looks at this aspect and suggests a five-point plan for getting started. It then considers some of the basic leadership skills that you will need to get the people for whom you are responsible to work well.

The book then looks at some of the particularly difficult situations you can face when managing for the first time –

managing former friends or colleagues, for example. It ends by looking forward to what you need to do to keep developing your leadership skills and effectiveness for the longer term.

managing your first 100 days – your 'honeymoon' period! 2

It is essential to have a plan, and to be absolutely clear what your goals are for your first 100 days. However busy you are, thinking things through, mapping out a plan and then regularly reviewing how you're doing will be essential to help you keep on top over the next three months. This isn't something where you can just wing it!

Setting your goals

Your goals should include:

- *what you need to learn.* If you are new to the organisation: what the company does, who does what, the competition, the business situation, the business plan, the politics, the culture, how the finances work, how things get done, who the key influencers are, key issues facing the organisation. Even if you are already in the company, you may not know all these things well enough for your new job. So make the most of this opportunity to ask questions, and make sure you really understand how the organisation works and where it's going before you embark on your new contribution to it.

■   *whom you need to meet.* Your list should include your boss, your team members, colleagues, key influencers, key customers, key suppliers. You should make contact with all these people, even if you were already in the organisation, to build relationships and position yourself in your new role.

▲   *what you need to achieve.* By the end of your first 100 days you should have found out what people expect from you and what are the key issues that you need to address. You should have started formulating your vision of what you want to do and how you're going to get there; and you should have made a good first impression.

Five-point plan for your first 100 days

The following simple five-point plan will help you achieve these goals:

1   Get to know your boss.

2   Invest in your team.

3   Develop relationships with key colleagues and customers.

4   Establish your credibility.

5   Decide and communicate your plans for the future.

Set yourself a clear timescale for achieving this.

You will find you seem to be spending a lot of time just talking and not doing anything, but this is OK – the more you get to know now the better things will go later on when you do start doing – so make the most of this opportunity to learn and think.*

'The most important thing is to have clear set of objectives.'

'Be absolutely clear what you are going to achieve each day – and especially your first day.'

'Your first meetings are critical – particularly with your team and your boss. Judgements are made! Just be yourself, talk straight, be enthusiastic, and you'll be fine!'

(* Throughout the book the remarks in italics are quotations from real-life experiences of managing for the first time.)

Step 1   Get to know your boss

Set up your first meeting with your own boss. He or she is best placed to help you map out your introduction plan, and help you position your role in the overall context of the business. Make sure you cover the following points in your meeting:

● What are your boss's objectives?

■ What does the boss expect from you – ie what do you need to do, how will you know you've done it well, what are the timescales?

▲ What are the key issues that need addressing now?

◉ What are your top learning priorities?

- Who are the key people you should meet first?

- Who are the most influential people?

- How do decisions get made?

- What are the potential pitfalls?

- Information about your team?

- When and how does the boss want to be updated?

- When do you need to get the boss's OK before you go ahead?

- What is really important to the boss?

- What really annoys the boss?

'Always do things that will help your boss reach their objectives first, and always support and never upstage or openly criticise your boss.'

'Have a crystal clear understanding of the expectations your new boss has of you. Make sure you get sufficient time from your new boss for feedback and coaching.'

'Understanding your boundaries and how you fit into the overall organisation strategy is critical. Starting a new job is exciting and it is easy to get carried away with your plans and to forget that some things may need your boss to say OK.'

'As a new manager you will be keen to please your new boss, but don't fall into the trap of saying yes every time. Agree your objectives, keep focused on these and don't be afraid to push back if you feel under pressure.'

Step 2   Invest in your team

Equally important is to meet with your team as soon as you can.

Before you start, think how they may be feeling. Having a new manager is a big change for them. They need quick reassurance that life with you in charge is going to be OK, because even if they are pleased to have you as their new boss, it's quite likely that they will be anxious too.

They may be concerned that you will bring in sweeping changes and upset their established way of doing things. They may worry that they won't be able to live up to your expectations or cope with the changes, and look stupid. They may be worried that you won't share the same values as them. However irrational this might seem to you, you have to respect it and acknowledge it.

There are stages that people go through in any major change situation. There are many versions of this, but the following six steps are typical:

Denial	refusal to acknowledge the situation
Regret	sadness at the loss
Anger	resentment at the change
Gloom	anxiety about the future
Acceptance	adapting to the situation
Transition	positive attitude to the change

Some of your team may still be in the early stages of this progression.

'For you, things look great – you are embarking on an exciting and important journey – management! Your drive and personal motivation are running at maximum levels, and you're on a mission to succeed and make a difference. But the people who report to you are not necessarily feeling the same way. It is easy to fall into the trap of assuming everyone else is behind you and driven by the same bug. Contain your enthusiasm and don't assume everyone has the same passions and ideas as you do.'

'Even if you say you don't plan to make quick changes they won't believe you – you need to put a lot of time into communicating what you are doing and planning to give them the security they need.'

Your first team meeting

So, meet with the people who report to you as soon as you can. First impressions stick, so it's important to put time into planning this meeting. If you haven't run many meetings before, see the tips on page 47. Make sure you:

- outline the aim of this meeting – which is to introduce yourselves and what you all do, and talk about how you are going to work together

- say that having a new manager can be very unsettling, and you expect some of them are feeling little anxious and uncertain about you taking over as manager. Reassure them that you won't be making any big or dramatic changes – or if that is what you have been brought in to do, tell them so up front. Emphasise that your key objectives to start with are to get to know them and their roles and to support them.

▲ run through the structure and ground rules for the meeting

● introduce yourself – give the same information that you will want them to give you; ie keep it brief – just your name, where you are from, where you live, where you worked before, and something you enjoy doing outside work

● ask them to introduce themselves. If it's a big team make notes, especially of each name – if you do it for everyone it won't look odd and you will avoid the risk of forgetting them! Be careful not to ask personal questions in public – eg 'Do you have children?' or 'Are you married?' You are concerned with work, and not everyone feels comfortable talking about personal things in a group.

● discuss the key issues facing the team. Start by asking if someone would like to throw out an idea, but have one up your sleeve just in case, eg 'One issue I picked up during my interviews which seemed pretty important is…'. For each issue, your aim is to identify the problem, the potential solutions, the barriers to solving it, and the implications if it doesn't get fixed.

■ ask what they feel you need to include in your objectives for the first 100 days

▲ outline your objectives for your first three months – acknowledging the ideas that have come from the team

◉ also say what you're not going to do in your first 100 days, so they can see the limits clearly and see that you are focused and know your priorities

◉ make notes of any actions you or others committed to, summarise these at the end, and make sure you deliver on them quickly.

◉ fix next meeting times. It's a good idea to have more frequent meetings at the start.

'Make it clear that you are going to be asking them lots of questions over the next few weeks, because you want to get to know them, and develop a good understanding of how things work and how it all fits together. So they will need to be patient with that and understand that if you ask about something, it's not because you want to interfere or change it – you just want to understand how they work, to help you be an effective manager and leader for them. If you don't say this, people can become defensive when you ask them things.'

'One boss I had handed round his CV at the first team meeting – it was a nice touch – open and honest.'

'Make them feel valued and show that you're genuinely interested in what they do.'

Subsequent team meetings

At your next meeting agree what the structure and ground rules for your team meetings will be so that people get to know how you will work together.

It is worth spending several meetings going through what the team does as a group, and how they do it. This means you all learn how things work (and it's surprising how much people don't know about the jobs other people do in many teams) and it gives you a chance then to step back and discuss as a team what works well and what could be done differently or better.

Your first one-to-one meetings

As well as team meetings you should have individual meetings with each person in your team. These are sometimes called 'one-to-ones'.

Here is a list of issues you may want to cover at the meeting. It may seem long, but you don't need to do it all at once! It covers most of the important things you need to know to understand what they do and gain an insight into current issues and what's important to them. This is useful information for you to manage them in the future – everyone is different, so it is important to find out what makes each individual tick, so you can manage each person as far as possible in the way they would like to be managed (rather than treating everyone the same or assuming everyone likes to be managed in the same way as you do). Before the meeting you might give them an outline of what you want to cover, so they can prepare beforehand:

- how long they have been in the organisation and in their present role
- what they did before this
- what their responsibilities and current goals are
- what they enjoy most
- what they enjoy least
- what they think they do best
- what they would like to do better
- their key challenges
- what they feel could be improved in the team
- what they think are the key issues for the team
- what motivates them
- what training they think they need
- what their long-term goals are
- what is important to them at work
- how they like to be rewarded
- what they are looking for from you as their boss
- how they would like to work with you.

Build an individual agreement with each of them on how you will work together. This might include how often they'd like one-to-ones, how they prefer to get information, what coaching and help they would like from you. Don't expect everyone to work like you!

'Take the time to find out what is important to people. Keep this in mind and try to organise things as far as you can to meet their needs. This will go a long way in motivating them to work well for you.'

'Spend time with and listen to your people – they have most of the answers.'

'One of the big challenges of becoming a manager is changing from hands-on doer to really finding time to spend with people. The bottom line is that you won't find the time – you will have to make it, schedule it – and make sure you stick to it.'

Step 3	Develop relationships with key colleagues and customers

Introduce yourself and get input from your customers – inside and outside – from suppliers, and from other key colleagues/ influencers. These meetings should cover:

- introducing yourself
- their role, how long they have been working in/with the organisation
- what they get from your team
- what is good and what could be better
- what they will be looking for in the future from you
- what they see as the top priorities in your area

■ who they would recommend you talk to – 'who can tell me about…'

▲ how to get things done (a subtle way of asking about the politics!)

● what things have gone wrong before, and why.

Asking the same questions of several different people ensures you get a balanced perspective on the issues you need to find out about. It also avoids you being led by what others choose to tell you – you control the agenda.

'Listen to your new peers and take the time to understand their opinions and views.'

'Show an interest in what's important to them. Try to understand their issues, priorities, and values.'

'Everyone knows you should make your boss look good. But few know the power of making your peers look good.'

'The best thing I did when I started was take time to get generally known by walking about and visiting each part of the business, so that people knew personally who I was. I got some brilliant informal inputs and really found out how the overall business works.'

'Treat everyone with respect – everyone has influence.'

Step 4   Establish your credibility – dos and don'ts

People will be sizing you up all the time in your first few weeks, so you need to be sure you make a good impression. Here are 10 tried and tested ways to gain respect in your new role – and a few things to avoid too!

1   Get some early wins or quick results

Do one or two things early on that have needed doing for some time, which are important or dramatic, or that lots of people will notice or benefit from. Show that you know how to do things well: set goals and deadlines, involve the right people, get the resources you need, deliver, communicate and recognise the achievement. Make sure you really understand the implications of making any early changes – so they are a guaranteed success!

'Every function has a couple of responsibilities which are really obvious to everyone in the organisation. Working in PR, the obvious choice for me is advertising – so I made my first objective doing a new press campaign. I brainstormed with the team, they came up with a great design for an advert and we did it within the first three months. People still talk about it, and that was over a year ago now.'

'Prove your added value, fast.'

2   Focus on the most important things

Identify the top three result areas and focus on these. Spend time proactively assessing and addressing things that limit or could improve productivity or effectiveness. Concentrate on the short term. This will keep everyone's energy levels high.

'New people can easily get lumbered with all the tasks other people want to avoid, and that nearly happened to me. It was only by prioritising ruthlessly, that I avoided being dumped on!'

3   *Deliver on commitments*

Meet *every* commitment you make. This is very important as people will then know they can always rely on you. Say no to the things you are not able to do at the point when the person asks you to do them – not later, when you find you're unable to meet them. If you do run into problems, let the person know as soon as possible and reset their expectations. Get disciplined at scheduling not only when things need to be done by, but also the time when they are going to get done. That way you're less likely to over-commit yourself.

'Show you can get things done. In every organisation there are different ways. I always focus on learning the short cuts, fast – it makes such a difference.'

4   *Demonstrate balance*

A lot of the challenge of managing and leading is keeping a balance between competing pressures. People will be assessing you on how well you are able to do this – particularly when you are new. For example, people will expect you to be:

visionary and creative	*and*	able to deliver and execute
decisive	*and*	open to others' input
focused	*and*	flexible
participative	*and*	able to make independent decisions
tough	*and*	fair

accessible	*and*	able to be detached
energetic	*and*	calm
ethical	*and*	streetwise
results-focused	*and*	good on process and with people

'Nothing is black or white – it's all about achieving a balance.'

5   Don't pretend you know things you don't

If you don't know, ask, or find out. Nobody can know everything they need to know, especially when they are new. If you start off trying to be perfect you will put yourself under a lot of unnecessary strain. And if you pretend, you'll probably get found out.

'People respect people for saying when they don't know something – it shows self-confidence.'

'I have a journalist friend who often feigns ignorance to get people to open up. It's called "naïve questioning". I tried it when I started managing this project team – it worked wonders!'

6   Admit mistakes

Everyone learns by their mistakes, and many of the things we learn that really stick are things we got wrong at the start and had to change. So, as the manager you have to set the example, and encourage an atmosphere where people feel comfortable doing things they haven't done before, taking risks and learning from mistakes.

'I actively admit mistakes, often, so it becomes the norm. I find if you do this, others will be willing to do the same and then you can all move on to more important things.'

7   Be confident, relaxed and positive

Keep things in perspective and always focus on the positive – what you *have* achieved rather than what you haven't. People expect a manager to show a positive lead, so you need to get your mindset trained to deliver on this.

'Humour is my best ally. I have a collection of silly gadgets in my drawer – if things get a bit serious I bring something out – instant diffusion!'

8   Communicate

Communicate lots. It's hard to over-communicate, especially at this stage.

'I just keep repeating the key points. And I make sure I put them across in different ways to make sure people have really understood them. I end up feeling like a parrot, but it certainly does the trick!'

9   Manage your emotions

You need to appear calm, level-headed, unstressed, and on top. Never let yourself get ruffled by things. You must show you can rise above personal feelings.

'Keeping your emotions in check can be tough, but is essential for long-term credibility.'

Chartered Institute of Personnel and Development

Customer Satisfaction Survey

*We would be grateful if you could spend a few minutes answering these questions and return the postcard to CIPD. <u>Please use a black pen to answer</u>. **If you would like to receive a free CIPD pen, please include your name and address.*** IPD MEMBER Y/N

....

1. Title of book ....

2. Date of purchase: month ....   year ....

3. How did you acquire this book?
☐ Bookshop   ☐ Mail order   ☐ Exhibition   ☐ Gift   ☐ Bought from Author

4. If ordered by mail, how long did it take to arrive:
☐ 1 week   ☐ 2 weeks   ☐ more than 2 weeks

5. Name of shop .... Town.. Country ....

6. Please grade the following according to their influence on your purchasing decision with 1 as least influential: (please tick)

	1	2	3	4	5
Title					
Publisher					
Author					
Price					
Subject					
Cover					

7. On a scale of 1 to 5 (with 1 as poor & 5 as excellent) please give your impressions of the book in terms of: (please tick)

	1	2	3	4	5
Cover design					
Paper/print quality					
Good value for money					
General level of service					

8. Did you find the book:

Covers the subject in sufficient depth   ☐ Yes   ☐ No
Useful for your work   ☐ Yes   ☐ No

9. Are you using this book to help:
☐ In your work ☐ Personal study   ☐ Both   ☐ Other (please state)

Please complete if you are using this as part of a course

10. Name of academic institution...

11. Name of course you are following? ....

12. Did you find this book relevant to the syllabus? ☐ Yes ☐ No   ☐ Don't know

Thank you!

To receive regular information about CIPD books and resources call 020 8263 3387.

1795/05/00

2

Publishing Department

Chartered Institute of Personnel and Development

CIPD House

Camp Road

Wimbledon

London

SW19 4BR

'I was too concerned to be liked when I first started, so I was too nice to everyone. Now I've got to make some changes, and people are feeling let down. I wish I'd been more contained.'

10   Manage work/home balance

Starting any new job is exciting, and it is easy to throw yourself into it body and soul. Sometimes there will be no choice but to put in extra effort to get up to speed, but watch out. How you act now will set people's expectations for the future. So start as you mean to go on.

'I have some rules which I make clear to everyone from the start – I do not work at the weekends and I do not do more than 10 hours a day. I think that's enough.'

'You are in this for the long term – it's a marathon, not a sprint.'

Things to avoid

When you start a new job in a new organisation, try to avoid:

● talking about your last organisation as if everything was perfect there, and isn't here

■ importing things that have worked for you elsewhere until you have got a good understanding of how things work here

▲ criticising other people – and especially your predecessor. This shows you up in a bad light and makes it awkward for people who used to work with him or her

- creating any enemies – or obvious favourites

- doing too much and getting overwhelmed and exhausted.

Step 5   Decide and communicate your plans

By now you will have learnt a lot, started building relationships, and will be formulating a clear vision of what you want to do based on the inputs of your team and all the other people you have talked to. You will know what the potential blocks are, who your supporters will be, and who you will need to work on. And you will have made a good first impression.

So now it's time to start acting. As with any project, map out where you want to get to and then work backwards to see what needs to be done to get there.

Don't be tempted into changing things too fast to make your mark. Unless you were brought in to make quick changes, take your time to make sure you have appreciated the implications of changing things and have got the buy-in and support you will need to make things successful. Three to six months is quite normal for this.

On the other hand, if there are changes to be made you can't leave it too long or you will look weak, and it will be more difficult to make the change. Again, it's all about balance.

Once you are clear on your goals and strategy you need to discuss and agree them with your boss and with your team.

You then need to communicate them to customers, colleagues, suppliers and key contacts.

'Go slow to go fast. Don't charge in with half-baked ideas, leave people behind, or set unrealistic expectations.'

'The key to success is to listen, gather lots of input and then make timely decisions. Remember to communicate to key stakeholders along the way – never blindside others – ie don't catch them unawares.'

'Make your vision as simple as possible without dumbing it down.'

'My test is – if I can't communicate my vision clearly to someone in less than five minutes and get their interest and understanding, then I'm not ready.'

'I begin with the end in mind.'

Get your boss's buy-in

Even if you have been talking regularly to your boss, you should have a special meeting to discuss and agree your plans. You may need to make a formal report or presentation, or you may feel a more informal talk will be more effective in getting your boss's input and buy-in – which is what you want to achieve.

In either case you should prepare what you want to say like a presentation, so that you have a good structure, and are ready to make the points clearly and simply. It is particularly important to:

- practise your opening statement – what you want to say, and how

- anticipate their objections and be ready with solutions to them.

'Emphasise that you really want your boss's input on your plans before you go any further – so that he or she feels involved and will support you.'

'Don't get annoyed or demoralised if he or she wants to change things. It's unlikely you'll get things 100 per cent right first time.'

Get your team's buy-in

Once you have acceptance from your boss, you need to agree an action plan with your team.

Your aim is to ensure that everyone in the team is clear what you want to achieve as a team, how you are going to do it, and who will be responsible for what – and that they all feel positive and responsible for making the plans work.

This is another critical meeting, so plan it carefully.

Start off by presenting the same as you did to your boss. You should have been talking regularly to your team, so the contents should not be a surprise. Ask for any comments/inputs, then move on to discussing how you will implement the plan.

If there are more than five in the team, divide them into small groups of three to four so you get maximum involvement.

Here's a discussion framework that can work well:

◉ What are the overall goals of our team?

◧ What are our highest priorities?

▲ What do we each think our role is in achieving those goals and priorities?

◉ Do others agree, or do they have different expectations?

◉ How do we each think our role should be measured – what does doing a good job mean?

◉ How do we each think others' roles should be measured/

◧ Who do we depend on to be successful?

▲ How are we going to communicate our plan?

'This process works well because everyone gets a say in the team's overall role priorities and measures, understands where they fit in, and appreciates how their role is viewed from the outside.'

It is easy in meetings like this to assume that everyone is 'on board', when actually they may not be, but are too shy to say so. So it's very important to flush out *any* concerns people may have before things get finalised.

A good way to do this is to ask questions in such a way that you really invite people to put their concerns on the table, rather than in a way that suggests you don't want any dissent:

Say:

'Does anyone have a problem with this?' – or to be even more open: 'Who has a problem with this?'	*rather than*	'Right, so does everyone agree then?'
'Is there anyone who feels uncomfortable with this approach?' – or, to be more open still: 'Who feels uncomfortable with this approach?'	*rather than*	'Is everyone on board then?'
Now what have we missed?	*rather than*	'Is that everything?'

After the team meeting, follow up with each person individually to consolidate and agree their role, goals and priorities, and how they will be measured. For tips on setting objectives, see page 37.

When you have met everyone individually, reconvene as a group for final reinforcement. Ask each person to run through their role, goals and priorities, making sure everyone's goals are clearly linked to the goals of the team as a whole, and to the overall aims of the organisation.

Take the team off site
If you can, try to hold your team meeting 'off site' – ie away from the office, or at least somewhere different from usual. This helps to create a special atmosphere, and gives people some space to think, free from the distractions of the office.

Try to include some kind of fun or social activity as well – a meal, a challenge or competition, silly games, or a team event like bowling or five-a-side. It is a great way to get people to 'gel', and is worth the time and money invested.

'I wish I had done a team-building day earlier in the set-up phase. When I eventually got around to it, it was an amazing experience and really brought out some fascinating learnings for all of us. Doing it earlier would have been more beneficial.'

Tell the world!
This is something you will have covered with your team, but make sure you have thought of every person who is affected by your plan or who may have an interest in what you do, so that you don't miss anybody. Use every appropriate communication channel. For people who are particularly affected/interested, communicating in person is the best, even if you back up with something written.

'Internal marketing is important. I believe that if you're doing great work it will be noticed. But I don't hesitate to blow our trumpet when the team is going well – you'll be surprised at how many things you assume are "visible" in your organisation may not actually be visible to others outside. It is difficult to over-communicate if the communication is justified.'

'Communicate to everyone affected.'

Management basics for your first 100 days

As you work through your first 100-day plan there are a number of fundamental management tasks and skills you will need to put into practice straightaway.

Don't worry about trying to be perfect straight off – these skills take time to develop, so just do what you can in the areas suggested.

Other books in this Management Shapers series will help you in detail on the individual skills you will need – leadership, decision-making, problem-solving, etc, so here we shall focus on just the key points and tips. The fundamental skill areas for a new manager are:

1   motivating your team

2   delegating responsibility

3   setting clear goals and objectives

4   giving constructive feedback

5   communicating effectively

6   managing meetings and team briefings

7   managing your time effectively

8   acting like a manager.

1 Motivating your team

A major first concern will be how to motivate your team. There is no single answer to this, as each person is different and individual. But, along with basic good management, the following generally have a good effect with most people:

- noticing birthdays, the anniversary of their start date, how they are feeling, how much work they have on

- saying thank you, noticing and recognising results and special efforts

- making them feel valued

- sharing experience and knowledge

- offering to help

- giving them space and respect

- being open to different approaches and solutions

- showing confidence in their abilities, and supporting them

- being honest and trustworthy

- ◎ not taking personal credit for their successes

- ◎ never blaming

- ◼ never criticising or being sarcastic

- ▲ making work fun.

'One useful thing I did was simply to invite one of the senior executives to a team breakfast meeting to talk informally about what we were doing and how things were going. It made the team feel important.'

'I make my recognition as individual as I can. The extra thought/ effort goes a long way.'

'I made a commitment to my team to have one-to-ones which I have maintained to this day. That one simple action has allowed me the opportunity to keep them at the forefront of anything that I do.'

'Never manage by threat – you'll be feared by the team and they won't be productive. They will worry every time they speak or do something and you'll have no team spirit.'

'Treat your team with respect as individuals – just because you're the boss it doesn't give you the right to treat people differently.'

2 Delegating responsibility

'Leading a team towards delivering on a vision/strategy is far different from "doing it yourself". This is a huge stumbling block for new managers. Many new managers get frustrated and default back to "doing it themselves".'

You need to understand enough to be able to go down into the detail if needed, so that you can:

- help
- understand if things aren't working
- account for how things are done in your area.

But you should delegate the 'doing' as far as possible.

If you get too involved in the detail you will have less time and less mental ability to step back and see where things are going. You have to make time for yourself to do the thinking and the planning, which is your job, and what is expected of you.

'Whenever something lands on my desk, my first thought is: "Who would be the best person to handle this?".'

How to delegate

When delegating, you need to think – how able is the person to do what I want them to do and how motivated are they to do it? The higher they score on both these elements, the more you can let them be free; the lower they score the more you need to help and direct them.

As far as possible, you should try to delegate things to people that they are either good at or enjoy doing.

Competent people will get things right 80 per cent of the time and can generally sort out their own problems. What they need from you is help, guidance and support.

'Give your people the trust and confidence to take their own decisions. But don't leave them exposed. Carefully make sure they are up to the task and invite them to ask for help without making them feel stupid.'

'Sometimes I have to bite my lip to give them a chance to solve it their way. I consciously limit myself to offering advice or guidelines, and never give a finished solution.'

'Remember, you're not going to be able to fix absolutely everything – it's called bandwidth! Wherever you can, empower your team to sort their own issues out – knowing they can escalate to you if they need to. It's a good learning process for them and shows you have confidence in them and trust them. If you try to sort everything out yourself, you'll end up being a dumping ground for everyone's issues.'

How to keep tabs without seeming like Big Brother

Delegation isn't giving up responsibility. One of the big challenges can be to keep track of what you have asked people to do without seeming like a control freak. However it is important to make notes and follow up with people – you may not do the work, but ultimately you carry responsibility for what your team does.

For each person, keep a 'bring forward' file of things to give them and things you have asked them to do, and which you need to know are completed, or you need to follow up on. A page in your personal organiser/notebook for each person is a practical way of doing this.

'I check through my list when I have updates. But I always get them to take the initiative in the update meetings – ie they tell me how things are going and I only ask something if I really need to know or if they have not mentioned it. Nobody likes feeling controlled.'

'Don't keep checking – encourage people to discipline themselves. Agree in advance when you want to have updates/drafts, etc, or simply ask them to confirm when things are done, or say if they are delayed.'

'Unless it's really important, I only make a deal of it if things get missed two or three times.'

3 Setting clear goals and objectives
People need to know the answers to these questions:

● What are my basic job responsibilities?

■ How will I know I am doing a good job?

▲ What are the additional goals I need to achieve over the next x weeks, and how will I know I've achieved them?

And most people want to be challenged.

There is much guidance around on how to set good objectives. The most common is the SMART checklist. This is a way of remembering that to be effective, any objective must be:

S   *specific* about what is to be achieved

M   *measurable* in quality and/or quantity

A   *agreed* by both sides

R   *realistic* and achievable in the time and with the resources available

T   *timed* to a deadline.

'Be as clear as you can about what you want them to do and the way you want it done.'

'I never assume people will know what standards I am expecting – they may have a completely different idea. If it is important, it does not go without saying!'

'I let people come up with their own objectives as far as possible, then we discuss and agree them. That way they are much more committed to them.'

4 Giving constructive feedback

People want and need to have feedback on how they are doing – both the good and the bad.

It's *how* you give feedback that is most important. All feedback must be constructive. This means that it aims to build on the good points and helps to improve the areas that need to be improved. Feedback is about maximising someone's performance. Demotivated people are not usually very productive, so feedback should always aim to leave the person feeling confident that they can improve/do what's required.

There are many books and courses on how to give feedback – and it can be useful to go on a course where you are video-taped to see how you come across. Here are some general tips:

'Give people more detailed feedback to start. That way they will get to know what you want and you will be able to leave them to get on with it in the confidence that they understand your expectations and standards.'

'Always give feedback as close to the event as possible.'

'Always give praise in public, criticism in private.'

How do you give praise without going over the top?
Being factual in giving praise not only helps the person understand *why* they did a good job, so they can repeat it, but also helps you not to go overboard with praise. For example,

'Rather than say "That was a great report", I say "Your report was well structured and just the right length".'

'I am careful to praise equally as far as I can to avoid creating divisions in the team.'

How do you let people know when you're not happy – and help them turn it round?
The key here is to focus on behaviour, not on personality. People can work on changing their behaviour, but personality transplants are a little harder…

Here is a good framework to use:

- Describe the behaviour – what you have observed.

- Describe the impact of this on you/the team/the other person – why it's not OK because of the consequences it has. Do not assume any reason, accuse, or make any judgement (eg don't assume that being late is because they are lazy).

- Ask how they see it – what happened.

- Make a suggestion or request – what is needed.

- Let them decide how to achieve that, then agree how you will move forward, and offer help.

- Follow up.

For example:

say	*rather than*
'I noticed you were angry with her.'	'You were pretty aggressive to her.'
'She seemed pretty upset.'	'You really upset her.'
'How did it happen?'	'Why did you do that?'
'How could you have handled that differently?'	'You shouldn't be so heavy handed.'

'She would probably appreciate it if you…'	'So what are you going to do about it, then?'
'I'd like you to…'	'You should…'
'How will you resolve this?'	'If this happens again…'

When giving negative feedback, always find something to praise – eg 'I liked the way you presented it – you really pre-empted their concerns.' Try also to offer help or reassurance if you can – eg 'Let's work on that together' or 'I find that hard too.'

'I never call it criticism, I call it observation. I ask how they think it went. Then I say "Can I make an observation?" or "I noticed that…".'

'Instead of saying "You didn't do a very good job at that", I ask "How else could you have done that?" That way they will realise for themselves they could have gone about it differently, which is much more acceptable than being told by someone else.'

'I find discussing training needs is a good way of getting people to talk about their weaknesses without seeming critical.'

'A mistake is a mistake, not a personal offence.'

'I've learnt that it's best to be straight and pull people up on small mistakes when they happen, rather than let them build into a mountain which ends up sending you into a blind rage.'

'Don't go over old mistakes – move on.'

People don't respect a boss who is always soft, and who doesn't have the courage to say if things aren't right.

'As soon as I feel things aren't going right, I think through to the end game. If you don't raise problems early on, it will be harder to do something later when it has got a lot worse and you're running out of patience. As well as being fair to the person by telling them when they're not meeting expectations, you're also giving yourself a route to take action later on if things don't improve. And I make sure I keep notes right from the start!'

'Have progress reviews on a regular basis – that way feedback becomes ongoing and there are no surprises when it gets to annual review time.'

Ask for feedback

You need to receive, as well as to give, feedback. Asking for feedback from your the people who report to you, and from your customers, is a good way of making sure you are in tune with what people are expecting of you. This isn't something you should do every day but it is a good thing to do whenever you are working on something important or whenever you have a one to one meeting. Frame it in terms of 'Is there anything else I can be doing for you – anything I'm not doing or could do better?'.

5 Communicating effectively

There are three main areas of communication you need to focus on from the outset:

● listening

▦ giving people the information they need

▲ involving people in decisions.

Listening skills
The key techniques are these:

Ask open questions	This gets people talking. Open questions start with 'What', 'Why', 'How', 'Tell me about…'.
Encourage	Have a relaxed posture, make eye contact, nod, smile, make encouraging comments – 'I see', 'Go on', 'Uh ha.'
Leave silences	Don't jump in if there is a pause – let the other person fill it.
Concentrate on listening	This means not talking yourself, not interrupting, not spending the time thinking what you are going to say next and just waiting for a chance to say it.
Probe	Dig down: 'Tell me more about…', 'Can you be more specific?', 'What do you mean by…?', 'What is the thinking behind…?'
Summarise/ paraphrase	Show that you have taken on board what they have said and check that you have understood correctly. Eg: 'You must have felt…','So it sounds as if…', 'Are you saying that…?', 'If I understand you correctly…'.

Giving people the information they need
'Communication is where most managers fall down – formal and informal communication must become constant and instinctive.'

Be as open as you can. Tell people as much as you are able about what's happening that is relevant to them and their jobs. At the end of each day, think about what has happened and what you need to communicate to the people who report to you, or to your boss or others who have an interest.

Use different methods, as needed. Written information/ e-mail or voicemail is fine for communicating facts.

Things that are more complex or emotive and that could be misunderstood should be explained in person. It can be so tempting to avoid talking to someone personally because it takes more time, and is more complex – but it saves time and trouble in the long term. People are much more committed to working with you or resolving issues if you talk to them personally– it's definitely worth the trouble.

There will be times when you have to keep things confidential, and this can make it hard. However, people respect that you have a responsibility not to divulging confidential information too soon. It is better to say 'yes, I do know what is being discussed but I am not able to talk about it yet' than to deny you know anything.

People will analyse everything you say for hidden meaning – so you really need to think through how it might be understood before you communicate anything important – it's amazing what people can read into the simplest statements!

'Nobody likes to hear things on the grapevine that they should have been told directly.'

'I say important things several times and in several ways to make sure they get across. Most things don't stick until someone has heard them seven times!'

'After one very bad experience, I never send negative feedback by e-mail or voicemail. It feels safe at the time but it is disastrous. Face-to-face is vital – people need to be able to see the colour of your eyes.'

If you have people on your team who are home based, or work part-time, or who are out on sick or maternity leave, make sure that they get as much information and feel as much a part of the team as everyone else. This means extra work for you, but it should not be overlooked.

'Set regular times for telephone updates, and stick to them.'

'Use technology as far as you can – have people teleconference in to team meetings; use e-mail/voicemail for updates.'

'My team is spread across five locations, three of them abroad. So I get them all together a few times a year – and I always build in time for some fun.'

Involving people

For every decision you make, you have a choice on how much to involve people – and you need to make the appropriate choice for each situation.

The full spectrum is:

- delegate the decision
- go for consensus
- consult the team and then decide
- consult a few individuals then decide
- decide and tell.

You should always make it clear how your decision will be made, and, especially if it's 'decide and tell', why.

'Being a manager is a constant balancing act between being participative and autocratic – how much can you practically involve people in decisions and how much do you just have to tell? For me, involving people is:

- *polite*
- *intelligent – utilising the intellectual assets around you*
- *effective – people will help execute something they have helped to design, and will help get you out of any mess because they helped create it.'*

6 Managing meetings and team briefings
Basic checklist

- ● Before every meeting, think 'What do I want to get out of this meeting, and what do the others want to get out of it?'

- ▣ Plan the agenda.

- ▲ Communicate the agenda and objectives before or at the start of the meeting.

- ● Start on time and end on time.

- ● Make sure everyone knows each other.

- ● Set the ground rules.

- ▣ State how decisions will be made.

- ▲ Nominate someone else to take notes/action points.

- ● If you are presenting, nominate someone else to take the role of facilitator/chair.

- ● Invite others to present things – don't feel you have to know and communicate everything.

- ● Keep moving through the agenda and don't let it stray off course.

- ▣ At the end summarise what has been agreed and what actions people have agreed to take and by when.

- ▲ Keep a flipchart/note of 'parked' issues – peripheral but important issues that come up during the meeting – and deal with them at the end.

'I once went on a training course where we all had to take it in turns to try to lead a brainstorming meeting, while the rest of the group had to be as disruptive as possible – phones went off, people went off to get a drink, interruptions all over the place – it was terrible! But it made me realise how important it is to state those basic ground rules at the start – or you can get decimated!'

Team briefings
How do you make sure that everyone in the team knows what they need or should know about what's happening in the team and what other people are doing? There are lots of different ways of doing this.

If you have a big team you might ask them to send you a weekly summary of achievements or issues for that week and key things coming up next week, and copy it to the rest of the team. If you create a template for this, it gives them a clear framework for writing what you want, is easy for you to assimilate into one report for your boss if you have to do this, and also means you limit how much they put down, so people don't spend too long on it.

Regular team meetings are essential. Use them to:

● give a business update and overall summary of key issues that have happened and are coming up. This is one of your prime responsibilities – to know what's happening in the company/organisation at large, what's happening with the competition/the world outside, and to communicate this to your team so they understand the big picture, the overall vision and strategy, and how they fit into it.

■ recognise individual achievements in front of everyone

▲ discuss issues that need a brainstorm, or everyone's input/support

● get one person each time to do a quick run through on something they are doing, that is of general interest. This helps people understand what others do, helps each individual crystallise key information about their job by having to explain to other people, and means people can cover for each other more easily.

● give a general update on what is going on. You need to be clear about what to include in team meetings to avoid that boring round-robin syndrome.

Every team has a common unifying purpose that brings everyone together, even if the individuals are all doing different things. For instance, our role is to provide x to y, to meet x revenue target, to develop x new product/service, achieve x customer satisfaction rating. Each individual's job and goals should be linked to that overall purpose or goal.

In meetings you should focus on things that are clearly linked to the common purpose or goal, so you maintain everyone's interest. Things that are not clearly linked to this should be dealt with separately or in individual discussions. Team meetings should be about team-relevant things.

Other good tips:

'You should have a mix of prescheduled meetings and impromptu ones when there are things that need to be communicated; otherwise they can feel too regimented.'

'There is an element of fun in every meeting I run. This should fit with the culture of the team. In my team everyone has a ghost portfolio of shares, including some company shares and at each meeting someone has to talk about their portfolio and how it has performed. This is fun and keeps them all focused on the stock price and how the company is doing against the competition.'

'I start every meeting with what we are trying to achieve. What are our top five objectives. Everyone should know the top three…in order.'

'I schedule meetings before lunch or at the end of the day so people are more focused on finishing on time. It works. I also ask people the day before if they have anything they want to put on the agenda. That gives me time to think how to handle issues in advance.'

'In the initial stages I led the weekly team briefings in order to set the tone, objectives and really build the momentum. However, now I am asking them to take over running these meetings to give them opportunities to learn about leadership and give them a true sense of responsibility. It also means they have a better understanding of what my role of leader means.'

'We spend time doing what the Spanish call 'conocimiento'. This means getting to know each other. We go round the room and check with each person how they are doing, what is going well, what they have had or are having difficulties with – it can be professional or personal. It helps the team to get to know how each person is feeling, encourages people to be open about things they find tough, *and sometimes raises important issues which affect the efficiency of the whole team. The time investment is well worth it.'*

'I watch more experienced people in meetings and learn from how they operate – when they choose to say something, when they let things go, how they phrase things. It's the best way to learn!'

7 Managing your time effectively

The key principles of effective time management become even more important when you have not just yourself but a group of other people to manage and take into account.

It's important to:

● be accessible, available when needed

■ be flexible/versatile to cope with change

▲ accept that you will have to let some things go.

Time management tips

● Tackle the hardest things first.

■ Allocate 20 per cent of your day – 1.5 to 2 hours – to making progress on your most important objectives. Otherwise all your time will go on reacting to things/ meetings and you will not meet your main goals.

▲ Have a maximum of three major things on the go at any one time.

● Add at least 20 per cent to any time estimate.

○ Bank similar things together – eg phone calls, e-mails, voicemails, and do them a reasonable number of times per day depending on your job requirements. It's easy to dart around responding to them in ones and twos, which is not so efficient.

○ Handle things once, or maximum of only twice.

■ Do one thing at a time, and keep your working space clear of other papers so you don't get distracted or tempted on to something else.

▲ Move through things quickly: don't keep checking.

○ Don't waste time perfecting things that don't have to be perfect.

○ Don't reinvent the wheel unnecessarily.

○ Treat time like money – spend it wisely.

■ Avoid becoming 'meeting-ed out'. Have meetings only when you need them – especially team meetings. Schedule them, but be flexible about shortening or cancelling them if there's no need at the time. Similarly, allow for unscheduled meetings when there *is* a need.

▲ Always let people know if you are not able to do something, rather than just leaving it.

'Identifying and then not losing sight of priorities is really important when you have so much to do.'

8 Acting like a manager

Being a manager is quite a change from being part of the team, and it can be hard to know how to handle it. So how do you act the part? Here are some typical questions and some suggested responses:

● *Should I get there first and leave last?* If you are always first in, it can make everyone else feel they have to be too. It's the quality of what you contribute – in your planning and direction – that counts, not the time you put in. You can arrive last and leave first if you meet – and preferably exceed – your commitments!

■ *Is it all right just to sit and think?* Definitely!

▲ *Do you have to live and model company values, even if they are not quite your own?* Representing the company viewpoint, culture, values, etc is part of your role as a manager. But don't become a stooge – people will see through you.

● *So how do you deliver company messages, even when you disagree with them?* You have a responsibility as a manger to be positive and professional in delivering company messages. However, if you do disagree, you can always say things like 'this view may be challenged by some, but it is the position the company has decided to take and which we will follow'. That way you are allowing for dissenters (of which you are one!), but you are not openly criticising the company. If you have concerns about your bosses' strategy, etc, they should be fed upwards not downwards.

- *Can I still go out and get drunk with my team?* Probably a bit risky!

- *What if I don't know the answer to something?* Managers are no longer 'heroes' who have to have the answers to everything. So you don't always have to be right, but you should know how to find out.

- *Do I have to dress differently?* No – do what you feel is comfortable for you in your environment. A friend of mine who became a manager went out and bought two suits to mark the transition – and they have been in the wardrobe ever since! Look at what other managers in your company do and follow company practice – or strike out on your own if you want to be different! Being dressed appropriately can help you to feel the part if you are having a wobbly day...

Much of how you act will depend on the culture of the organisation you work in – there is no one right answer. But in general, try to be true to yourself – not just for your comfort, but also because one of the things people look for in a manager is consistency and predictability. So they need to get to know how you operate as part of building their trust in you.

Managing typical challenges for the first-time manager

So far we have looked at your goals and strategy for your first 100 days, and covered some of the key management skills that you will need to put into practice early on. But there are some particular challenges that are common for the first-time manager: you are quite likely to find yourself in the difficult position of having to manage people who are:

- friends or colleagues
- peers in the same team
- older than you
- more experienced or expert than you
- different from you
- against you.

Managing these situations, especially for the first time, can seem a bit daunting.

As with most things in management, preparing in advance and being sensitive and respectful in the way you go about things will get you a long way.

You will probably find that people 'try you out' to see how you are going to cope with your new role. Even people whom you thought were your friends will change in relation to your role. They will want to test your authority – to see if you can be tough, say no, or push back. Whether they were friends or colleagues before, and whether they are young or old, new or experienced, they need a manager to lead and guide and support them. That person is now you – and you need to show that you are going to be good at this job.

Don't be scared about being tough. If you start off being too nice it's hard to get tough, but if you start off being tough, being nicer will always be a positive. People want a leader to be strong and decisive.

'You need to be willing to make a stand. There is more respect in taking a well-thought out position than to move back and forth in that grey zone of trying to please and appease everyone.'

'People will always rail against an authority figure.'

Managing friends or colleagues

Getting the right mix of friendliness/familiarity with friends or colleagues can be difficult for both sides. You may feel uncomfortable asking them to do things, or telling them if you're not happy with something. They may worry about disagreeing with you, or giving you feedback when they're not happy.

It is good idea to get it out in the open so everyone knows where he or she stands. Some managers find it helpful to have a discussion about it – ask the team how they feel about it, and what everyone's expectations are, and then build an agreement about how you will work together.

Others just make it clear that there may be times when there are tough decisions to be made, or things go wrong, or you disagree. If that does happen, work issues will take priority and neither of you should take things personally or feel you should treat each other differently than anyone else.

You should still be yourself, but remember you now have a new role to play, and this has to come first at work. You may need to be more cautious.

If you used to be friends and share problems with someone on the team it may be tempting to continue, but this could put both of you in an awkward position, and could spoil the friendship.

People may try to catch you off guard outside work – but however much they may bait you, you need to be vigilant not to let anything slip out that shouldn't.

'I make sure people know where they stand. I say things like "I'm talking to you as your manager" so they know what the situation is.'

'Sometimes, the only way is to separate work and outside relationships.'

'One of the sacrifices you may have to make is in relationships you have with people outside the workplace. You will have to step back a bit, keep your emotions in check, be less familiar and less involved.'

'Sometimes it won't be appropriate to go along to things anymore, or you won't get invited – and this can be hurtful. Suddenly you are perceived differently. Try not to take it personally – after all, you

probably wouldn't choose to go out drinking with your boss on a Friday night either!'

'You just have to accept that people bitch about their boss – it's a fact of life. So however well you get along, that's the score.'

Here's how one manager handled a tricky situation:

'One of the first things that happened to me was a guy in the team whom I often used to go drinking with called in 15 minutes late on my third day and left a message to say he was taking a day's holiday. This disrupted the whole day's work schedule. When he came back I had a discussion with him which resulted in a disciplinary and recorded oral warning. This was not an easy decision, but was absolutely the right thing to do. It did not make me popular for a few days but in terms of clearly defining my seriousness in pursuing the change from "worker" to "manager", the message was clear.'

Managing peers in the same team

As a first-time manager or team leader you often have to wear two hats. Half of you is doing a job as part of the team and the other half is having to manage the team and do tough things like delegating and managing performance. So you're split between being friend and foe – not fully part of the team, but not detached either. Again, you should discuss this with the team.

'I coped with this by linking up with someone else who is in a similar situation. That way we shared experiences, bounced ideas off each other, and used each other as a sounding-board for resolving issues. It was my saving!'

Managing people who are older than you

It can be a bit daunting telling someone who is your parents' age what to do, but that is your role and that is what they expect from you. The key thing here – as with all your people – is respect. Older people will have more work experience and more life experience than you, so make the most of this.

The best way to counter any feeling that you are going to be a threat or an upstart is to ask them for their views, and use their experience. They will appreciate it – everyone likes to feel valued. You will also make much better informed decisions as a result.

You may worry or find that older/more experienced people will expect you to follow their advice, because they are older/ wiser. For this reason you need to be very clear in every situation how your decision will be made. Tell them at the start whether you are seeking agreement/consensus, or whether you are you consulting them and getting their input before you a decide what to do. That way they will have the correct expectation about their input, and will more easily accept if you make independent decisions that are different.

Watch your language. Saying things like 'What would you do if…?' and 'What would you advise?' will suggest that you are asking them for their lead. Saying things like 'Have you experienced this before? What happened, and what was the result?' or 'What are the key issues here?' will sound more like fact-gathering.

Be careful not to accept everything unconditionally, or reject, everything that is put forward. Be prepared to give way on minor points, but for major issues if you don't agree, then say thank you for the input and you'd like to think it over some more.

'*Keep a balance between asking for their opinion, and giving them independent direction to justify your position as the boss. You need to be open, but not wet.*'

'*Never gloat. However pleased you are with how things have gone, nothing annoys people more. Even a hint of arrogance or cockiness and they will hate you.*'

One sales manager I work with told me about the first performance review he had to do, with an engineer older than his father who'd been with the company 23 years:

'*I'd just been on a great graduate sales training programme learning how to handle customer objections, so I handled all the negatives that came up in the performance review meeting like customer objections – ie never acknowledge the negatives, just build on the positives. So when he said "You're a great manager, but too demanding", I said, "So what makes me such a great manager?" Well, I came out feeling great, but later overheard him say, "It was like talking to a trained monkey." That made me learn that, however nervous you feel, the most important thing is to trust in yourself. Don't try to manipulate people, don't just put theories into practice, and don't be afraid to show your weaknesses.*'

Managing people who are more experienced or more expert than you

Many of the things that apply to managing people who are older than you also apply to managing people who are more experienced than you.

A good manager needs to surround him or herself with talented people. Ideally the individuals in the team will each be more expert at what they do than the manager is if the overall goals of the team are to be achieved.

It may feel a bit risky, but it is actually essential to have, hire and develop people who are better than you, and who will keep at the leading edge of what they do. It also means you can focus on your job of being the manager.

So rather than being afraid of people who are more experienced or more expert than you, you should actively seek them. Then your job is to act as their ambassador, help them achieve their goals, and celebrate their successes.

Where possible you should try to keep sufficiently up to speed on developments in their subject to be able to keep pushing the envelope forward. Drop the odd comment to show you are keeping yourself in the picture!

Remember, just because you want to be a manager, it doesn't mean everyone else wants to be one too. Many people prefer an 'individual contributor' job because it means they can focus on doing what they are good at doing. Others will have different priorities in their life which mean they don't want the unpredictability or responsibility of a management job. So, unless they applied for your job and didn't get it, they want you to be the manager.

'The most important thing is to hire good people.'

'I actively spend time with my best performers, and make sure I am doing everything in my power to help them succeed and grow.'

'The secret is to find ways to add value to your people. Find out what they are struggling with and see if you can help them overcome the obstacles. You don't have to know more about everything. You have to know enough to ask penetrating questions. You then "go in to bat" for them when they need you to. Make your people successful. That's what they want from you.'

Managing people who are different from you

It is more comfortable to be surrounded by people with the same background, values and lifestyle as you. But a team of clones is rarely effective.

Smart managers look for a mixture of skills and talents. Management experts, such as the famous British professor Belbin, have proven time and again that the most effective teams are teams that have people with a broad spread of skills and characteristics. For example, you need people who are good at coming up with (and challenging) ideas, people who are good at putting ideas into practical plans, people who are good at making plans happen, people are good at making sure all the details get followed up and closed down properly, people who have good contacts and are good at communicating to the outside world, people who are good team players, people who are good at managing other people. Most people have a mixture of different skills, some stronger than others, and the skill of a manger is to make sure that within the team all these aspects are covered and balanced, as far as possible.

Having a mix of backgrounds, values and outlooks in the team is also valuable, as it generally means the team is more creative and produces better results than a team where everyone has the same outlook.

Your responsibility as the manager is to make the individuals who make up the team gel and succeed together as a team, and to help them overcome any prejudices they may have about each other. At the same time you want to manage each person in the way that is going to make him or her most successful as far as you can within the team framework. The key is to keep an open mind, never judge or prejudge, but accept and maximise the benefit of the different contributions people in the team bring to you.

'The hardest part is managing people who are difficult or different from you. These people will demand a lot of your time and energy. But as a manager you cannot dismiss their needs just because you do not like their attitude or personality.'

'I found it very helpful (a bit late in the day) to realise that other people make different decisions and make decisions in different ways, but that doesn't necessarily mean theirs are right and mine are wrong or vice versa. There are different ways of doing things.'

'One of the hardest things I did was my first recruit. I had a choice between someone I felt really comfortable with because he'd done the same course as me at university, and another who was completely different from me – opposite sex, different ethnic background, city not rural background – so completely outside my experience. A friend who is an HR manager helped me think through what it was I needed in the team and what was important for the job, and when I looked at it objectively, it was clear that this person was the best fit for the job – even though I just didn't feel I would know how to deal with her. She has turned out to be the best person in my team, and the customers think she's great. In fact, managing her has been really enjoyable as I have really had to think and have learnt lots more than I would have otherwise.'

Managing people who are against you

Becoming a manager can be an unpopular move. There may be people out there who are jealous, resentful or worried that you becoming manager is going to have a negative impact on them. Some of them may be out to get you! To a certain extent you just have to accept this as part of the package, and try not to take it personally – hard as that may be! But if there are specific individuals whom you know have a problem, it is worth taking some time to try to build bridges with them.

There's no single prescription that is going to dissolve conflict situations, but there are some easy-to-learn techniques that can help. Applying the listening and feedback techniques described earlier are helpful here. Here is the model my company uses to train managers in dealing with conflict:

1 Ask the other person how they feel about the situation.

2 Don't react with your own opinion – just paraphrase/ summarise what you heard to check you have understood and show you are taking their view on board – eg 'What I'm hearing is…', 'I can understand your feeling that way.'

3 Probe why they feel as they do/try to go deeper.

4 Say what you feel and why, and check that they have understood – 'How does that sound to you?'

5 Suggest/ask for ideas for a solution that would meet both your needs –'Is there a way we can accommodate both…and…?'

6 Try to build small agreements. Focus on those rather than on the disagreements.

'I made a critical remark to a colleague and ended up in major conflict situation. Using this technique helped us to resolve it – and it really made me realise the importance of thinking about how you structure and say things – it makes such a difference.'

Keeping motivated

Learning about the organisation, building relationships, making a good impression, formulating an action plan, putting basic management skills into practice, and dealing with tricky management situations all at once can at times seem a bit much. Don't worry – it's common to feel overwhelmed with so many challenges and things to do. Just take each day at a time and keep focused on your objectives. Here are some things to help you keep on top.

Track your progress

Slow down and take stock. Track your progress against your objectives and do a mini self-appraisal at regular intervals. Ask yourself:

- How am I doing against my goals?

- Where am I doing well?

- How can I build on that?

- Where could I do better?

- How could I do better?

- Am I enjoying it? If not, how can I change that?

- Do I feel confident? If not, what do I need to do to change that?

- What have been my best successes so far?

- What have been my biggest learning points so far?

Get a mentor

Get external input, too, from people who are independent or who are committed to helping you succeed – advice and perspective from outsiders can be invaluable.

Many new managers find having a mentor helpful on an ongoing basis. This can be someone in the organisation, a colleague, or a friend – or somebody outside.

Some use a professionally trained coach/consultant as a 'role consultant' to help manage the challenges of a new management position.

It is definitely a good idea to have someone you can go to as a 'sounding-board', and for advice and guidance as you develop in your role.

'I kept in touch with my first boss and I still call her sometimes to ask for advice if I'm facing something really tricky.'

Look after your own well-being

Don't neglect yourself in this focus on managing others! Keep yourself balanced and healthy. You may want to keep your subject knowledge refreshed every now and again, so you don't lose the enjoyment of your old subject matter – even if you have now moved into a different role where you are spending time on management tasks rather than using your original skills.

setting yourself up for long-term success: building your manager toolkit

Much about being a good manager is the ability to cope with whatever happens and, more importantly, being competent at taking a leadership role in getting issues sorted out. Even the best managers find that they rarely have a day when they manage to do exactly what they had planned to do, because things tend to happen which throw plans off course.

As a manager, you have to be ready to handle not only the unexpected things that crop up for you personally, but also the things that happen for your team, or individuals in your team. Things like some work not getting done as planned, people leaving or going off sick when you're in the middle of a really busy patch, people in the team not getting on, the business situation suddenly changing and affecting what you all do, and so on. These things will all happen – you just don't know when!

There are, however, a number of things that, as a manager, you *can* predict.

We started the book with a list of some of the main tasks you will need to be able to perform as a manager – and we have looked at some of the more general underlying skills that you will need to develop so that you can do these tasks well.

It is a good idea to develop a plan to equip yourself to do the tasks you feel you don't know how to do, and to develop the underlying skills where you think you could learn to do better. In this way you will be better prepared to handle things that will probably, or definitely, happen at some point.

Many management skills can be learnt by observing what other people do and reflecting on how you would deal with similar situations. Watching business TV programmes, reading relevant books or magazines, or going on external training courses, can be helpful. The IPD Management Shapers series covers all the main management skills.

Key management skills you need to develop

The saying 'It's not what you do, it's the way that you do it' is particularly true for managers. So as well as learning how to do the tasks of being a manager, you also need to learn and practise how to deliver them well. It is mostly about interpersonal skills and communication.

Some of these skills may come naturally to you, others will need to be learnt and practised until they become natural. The main ones are:

- *Coaching skills* – being skilled at helping people to solve their own issues, rather than jumping in and taking over

- *Consensus building* – reaching decisions that all will respect, support and implement, even if they do not agree with them

- *Negotiating* – achieving what you want by being assertive rather than aggressive

- *Managing conflict* – managing disagreement between you and someone else, and between members of your team; one of the most telling signs of a good manager is how he or she handles conflict

- *Presentation skills* – being able to present an argument or information clearly and convincingly, one-to-one, in large groups, to management, customers, peers and employees

- *Written communication skills* – knowing how to write standard business documents for your organisation – business plans, project proposals, organisation plans, job descriptions, budget proposals, presentations, reports, action plans, etc.

Nobody expects a superhero!

It's important to remember that only the superhuman have all this competence off to a tee – so don't try to be Mr/Ms perfect! Just maximise your strong areas and make sure you devote some time to developing your competence in the areas you find more of a challenge.

Developing your leadership skills

At the opening of this book we talked about the two aspects of being a manager – the tactical, operational side, and the more strategic leadership side.

A lot of your focus to start with will be on the tactical, ie on *what* you have to do as a manager. But as you grow into your new role you will find yourself focusing more and more on fine-tuning *how* you carry out your role, and the impact your behaviour has on the motivation of others around you.

You may find yourself noticing more how others go about their role, and observing little tricks and techniques that make them effective in motivating people to follow them. In fact, copying the behaviour of leaders who just seem to get it right is a very effective way of developing your skills!

We all have experience of being managed – by our parents, teachers, political leaders, managers, and leaders in other activities. So sit back for a few minutes, and reflect on who your best managers and leaders have been, and why. Then ask some of your friends for examples of what they think makes a good leader. Here are some suggestions.

What makes a good leader?
- *Paint a clear vision*
  Provide clear direction
  Set clear strategy and objectives for achieving it
  Keep the team focused on getting things done.

■ *Be charismatic*
Inspire and motivate
Be enthusiastic and positive.

▲ *Lead by example*
Be competent and effective
Demonstrate ethical values – especially honesty
Show integrity
Rise above personal feelings and politics
Take risks, be innovative.

● *Make sound decisions*
Be balanced
Read situations perceptively
Utilise information and advice available.

● *Honour your commitments*
Do what you say you are going to do
Keep promises.

● *Be a facilitative leader*
Coach
Help people to achieve their goals
Empower
Be a good listener
Be supportive, give confidence
Be available, approachable, accessible when needed
Bring out the best in people
Help find effective solutions/fixes.

■ *Gel the team*
Create a good team spirit
Ensure all are aligned with the organisation objectives
and vision
Promote the team and its contribution to the
organisation
Provide a good working environment.

▲ *Communicate*
Listen
Make sure people know what's going on
Get input
Be open to ideas
Give feedback – good and bad.

● *Recognise achievement*
Notice what people have done
Reward contributions appropriately.

● *Manage change effectively*
Make change positive and exciting
Be flexible and adaptable.

While some of these skills are about how you are as a person,
many of them are behaviours that can be learnt over time.
As you develop your career you will pick up some techniques
and good approaches to typical management situations. By
putting them into practice yourself you will find out what
works for you. It often takes several attempts to get things
right and to feel comfortable – it's a case of practising these
skills until they become second nature.

The most important thing is to keep developing. Nobody is perfect at all aspects of being a manager – simply because no situations are ever the same when you are dealing with people. You can only apply the best judgement and skill you can, based on your learning, your experience and your observation of others – and always being open to suggestions and advice from others. So long as you do that, you should find that you cope with most situations.

Being a manager and a leader of other people is a challenge, and a responsibility – and also a privilege that you have been given.

Go for it!

further reading

ALBRIGHT M. *and* CARR C. *101 Biggest Mistakes Managers Make: And how to avoid them.* Hemel Hempstead, Prentice Hall, 1997.

CIAMPA D. *and* WATKINS M. *Right from the Start: Taking charge in a new leadership role.* Cambridge, MA, Harvard Business School Press, 1999.

See also the list of titles in this series, Management Shapers, on page vii. Further information is available from the CIPD (see details on page ii).

With over 105,000 members, the **Chartered Institute of Personnel and Development** is the largest organisation in Europe dealing with the management and development of people. The CIPD operates its own publishing unit, producing books and research reports for human resource practitioners, students, and general managers charged with people management responsibilities.

Currently there are over 160 titles covering the full range of personnel and development issues. The books have been commissioned from leading experts in the field and are packed with the latest information and guidance to best practice.

For free copies of the CIPD Books Catalogue, please contact the publishing department:

Tel.: 020 8263 3387
Fax: 020 8263 3850
E-mail: publish@cipd.co.uk
Web: www.cipd.co.uk/publications

Orders for books should be sent to:

Plymbridge Distributors
Estover
Plymouth
Devon
PL6 7PZ

(Credit card orders) Tel.: 01752 202 301
Fax: 01752 202 333

Other titles in the *Management Shapers* series

All titles are priced at £5.95 (£5.36 to CIPD members)

The Appraisal Discussion

Terry Gillen

Shows you how to make appraisal a productive and motivating experience for all levels of performer. It includes:

- ● assessing performance fairly and accurately

- ■ using feedback to improve performance

- ▲ handling reluctant appraisees and avoiding bias

- ● agreeing future objectives

- ● identifying development needs.

1998 96 pages   0 85292 751 7

Asking Questions

Ian MacKay

(Second Edition)

Will help you ask the 'right' questions, using the correct form
to elicit a useful response. All managers need to hone their
questioning skills, whether interviewing, appraising or simply
exchanging ideas. This book offers guidance and helpful
advice on:

- using various forms of open question – including probing,
  simple interrogative, opinion-seeking, hypothetical,
  extension and precision etc

- encouraging and drawing out speakers through
  supportive statements and interjections

- establishing specific facts through closed or 'direct'
  approaches

- avoiding counter-productive questions

- using questions in a training context.

1998 96 pages   0 85292 768 1

Assertiveness

Terry Gillen

Will help you feel naturally confident, enjoy the respect of others and easily establish productive working relationships, even with 'awkward' people. It covers:

- understanding why you behave as you do and, when that behaviour is counter-productive, knowing what to do about it

- understanding other people better

- keeping your emotions under control

- preventing others' bullying, flattering or manipulating you

- acquiring easy-to-learn techniques that you can use immediately

- developing your personal assertiveness strategy.

1998 96 pages   0 85292 769 X

Constructive Feedback

Roland and Frances Bee

Practical advice on when to give feedback, how best to give it, and how to receive and use feedback yourself. It includes:

- using feedback in coaching, training, and team motivation

- distinguishing between criticism and feedback

- 10 tools of giving constructive feedback

- dealing with challenging situations and people.

1998 96 pages   0 85292 752 5

The Disciplinary Interview

Alan Fowler

This book will ensure that you adopt the correct procedures, conduct productive interviews and manage the outcome with confidence. It includes:

- understanding the legal implications

- investigating the facts and presenting the management case

- probing the employee's case and diffusing conflict

- distinguishing between conduct and competence

- weighing up the alternatives to dismissal.

1998 96 pages   0 85292 753 3

Leadership Skills

John Adair

Leadership Skills will give you confidence, guidance and inspiration as you journey from being an effective manager to becoming a leader of excellence. Acknowledged as a world authority on leadership, Adair offers stimulating insights on:

- recognising and developing your leadership qualities

- acquiring the personal authority to give positive direction and the flexibility to embrace change

- acting on the key interacting needs – to achieve your task, build your team and develop its members

- transforming such core leadership functions such as planning, communicating and motivating into practical skills that you can master.

1998 96 pages   0 85292 764 9

Listening Skills

Ian MacKay

(Second Edition)

Improve your ability in this crucial management skill! Clear explanations will help you:

● recognise the inhibitors to listening

■ listen to what is really being said by analysing and evaluating the message

▲ interpret tone of voice and non-verbal signals.

1998   80 pages   0 85292 754 1

Making Meetings Work

Patrick Forsyth

Will maximise your time (both before and during meetings), clarify your aims, improve your own and others' performance and make the whole process rewarding and productive. The book is full of practical tips and advice on:

- drawing up objectives and setting realistic agendas

- deciding the who, where, and when to meet

- chairing effectively – encouraging discussion, creativity and sound decision-making

- sharpening your skills of observation, listening and questioning to get your points across

- dealing with problem participants

- handling the follow-up – turning decisions into action.

1998 96 pages   0 85292 765 7

Motivating People

Iain Maitland

Will help you maximise individual and team skills to achieve personal, departmental and, above all, organisational goals. It provides practical insights into:

● becoming a better leader and co-ordinating winning teams

■ identifying, setting and communicating achievable targets

▲ empowering others through simple job improvement techniques

◉ encouraging self-development, defining training needs and providing helpful assessment

◉ ensuring that pay and workplace conditions make a positive contribution to satisfaction and commitment.

1998 96 pages   0 85292 766 5